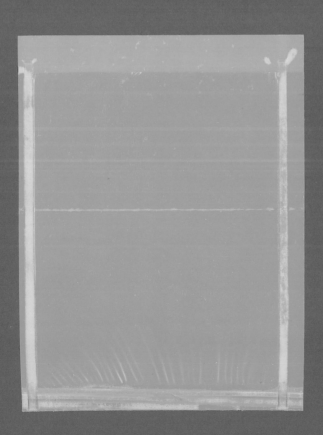

LOOK INSIDE

A TUDOR MEDICINE CHEST

BRIAN MOSES

Illustrated by Adam Hook

WAYLAND

Editor: Jason Hook
Designer: Ian Winton

First published in 1997 by Wayland Publishers Ltd,
61 Western Road, Hove, East Sussex BN3 1JD, England

British Library Cataloguing in Publication Data
  Moses, Brian. 1950-
Look inside a Tudor medicine chest
  1. Medicine - Great Britain - History - 16th century -
Juvenile literature
  I. Title II. A Tudor medicine chest
  610.9'41
ISBN 0 7502 1958 0
Printed and bound in Italy by G.Canale & CSpA, Turin.
Colour reproduction by Page Turn, Hove, England.

Cover Pictures: Anatomy lesson, 1581(c); surgical
implements(t); a toad(l); *Mary Rose* medicine chest(r).

Picture Acknowledgements: The publishers would like
to thank the following for permission to publish their
pictures: (t=top; c=centre; b=bottom; l=left; r=right)
British Museum 6b; Bruce Coleman/Hans Reinhard 13t,
/Jane Burton 16tr, /Alan Stillwell 16br, /John Markham
27br, /Nigel Blake *cover* bl, 29t; Bridgeman Art
Library/Glasgow University *cover*, /Giraudon 6c, /St
Kenelm Church 8bl, /British Library 9b, /Prado 18b,
/Biblioteque Nationale 22b, /Barber's Hall 25b,
/Unterlinden Museum 28t; Chapel Studios/Zul Mukhida
19t; Mary Evans 4c, 5t, 7, 8t, 9t, 18t, 20b, 22c; Houses
and Interiors 12t, 27t, 31; Hulton Getty 10c, 12c, 13c,
14l, 14tr, 16l, 21t; Image Select/Ann Ronan 11b, 19b,
24t, 24bl, 25t, 25c, 26, 29r; Mary Rose Trust *cover* br,
4t, 6t, 10t, 13b, 14br, 23b; Museum of London 8br;
NHPA/Stephen Dalton 4b, 10b, 17, 27bl; Oxford
Scientific Films/Rodger Jackman 15; Science and
Society Picture Library *cover* t, 5b, 12b, 20t, 21b, 23t,
24br, 28b, 30; Topham 22t; Wellcome Institute Library
11t, 20c, 29bl; Zefa *cover* background.

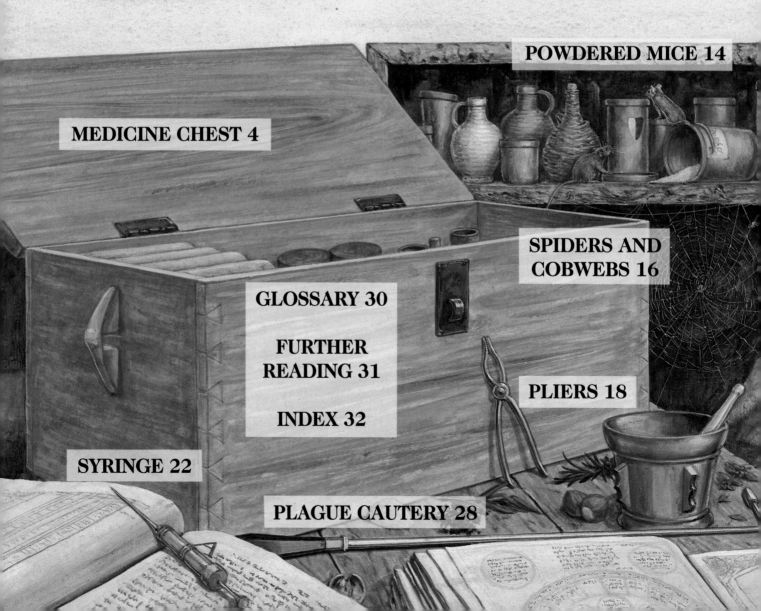

CONTENTS

MEDICINE CHEST

DIRT AND DISEASE

Take a look inside a Tudor medicine chest. Thick ointments ooze from pottery jars. Bunches of sweet-smelling herbs hang over a collection of strange tools: saws and scalpels, blood-stained bowls, a wooden mallet, flasks of yellowed glass and a brass syringe. What were all these things used for?

▲ This surgeon's medicine chest was found on the *Mary Rose*, Henry VIII's warship which sunk in 1545.

Five hundred years ago, people knew little about health and hygiene. In overcrowded towns you would see rats and flies swarming around the filth and dung that flooded the streets. People drank water from rivers full of sewage. Not surprisingly, disease spread quickly.

▲ A street in Tudor London.

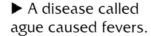

▶ A disease called ague caused fevers.

◀ Germs were spread by the many rats.

If you had lived in Tudor times, you would have washed a lot less than you do today. Queen Elizabeth I bathed regularly – at least once a month! Most people disguised dirt and body odours by using plenty of make-up and perfume.

A BOOK of TUDOR CURES

To cure a headache, press a hangman's rope to your head.

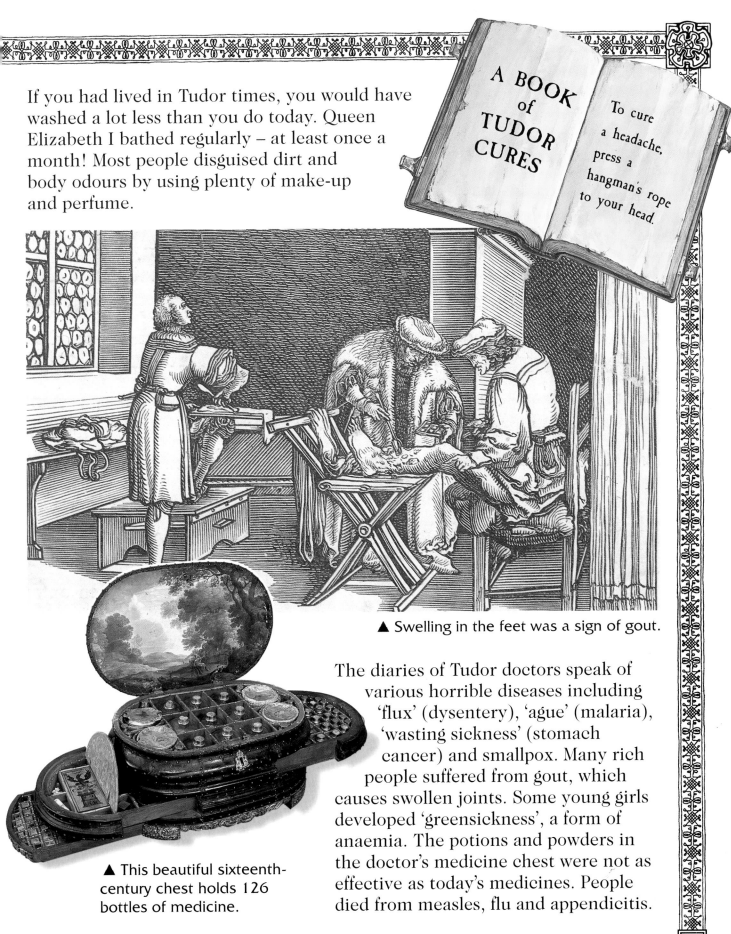

▲ Swelling in the feet was a sign of gout.

▲ This beautiful sixteenth-century chest holds 126 bottles of medicine.

The diaries of Tudor doctors speak of various horrible diseases including 'flux' (dysentery), 'ague' (malaria), 'wasting sickness' (stomach cancer) and smallpox. Many rich people suffered from gout, which causes swollen joints. Some young girls developed 'greensickness', a form of anaemia. The potions and powders in the doctor's medicine chest were not as effective as today's medicines. People died from measles, flu and appendicitis.

DOCTOR'S HAT

▼ The surgeon's hat from the Mary Rose.

SURGEONS AND QUACKS

The medicine chest belongs to a surgeon. He takes out the velvet hat which shows he belongs to a society called the Guild of Barber Surgeons. As he fastens its straps, he listens to a servant describe his master's symptoms – fever, pains in the liver and mad ravings. The surgeon shakes his head sadly. Many rich people have died this year from the terrible 'sweating sickness'.

▲ Tudor surgeries were unhygienic – look at the cat!

▲ A 'touch coin' from the reign of Henry VIII.

There was no National Health Service in Tudor times. A doctor's visit cost you a gold coin called an angel. This was too costly for many people, who had to rely instead on their own traditional herbal cures. Some coins were used more directly to treat illness. 'Touch coins', which had been touched by the king, were believed to cure 'scrofula', a disease which caused swollen glands.

If you were ill, you could visit one of three types of doctor – an apothecary, physician or surgeon. Apothecaries prepared and sold medicines, rather like today's chemists.

To cure gout, boil a red-haired dog alive in oil until it falls apart. Then add worms, hog's marrow and herbs. Apply the mixture to the affected parts.

◀ An apothecary's shop in 1505.

Physicians had studied ancient Greek ideas about medicine at university. They sometimes prescribed cures without even seeing their patients. The first surgeons were barbers, who performed operations as well as cutting hair! They became known as barber surgeons. If you needed a leg amputated, a wound treated, a tooth pulled or some medicine, you simply visited the barber.

Because doctors were so expensive, and their treatments so brutal, many people preferred to trust 'quacks' – travelling salesmen who sold their useless pills, potions and powders as miracle cures for diseases. One such disease was the strange 'sweating sickness' which killed many rich people in the years after 1485, but vanished in 1581.

▶ A quack selling cures in about 1600.

URINE FLASK

GIVING A SAMPLE

The next patient is a feverish old sailor, who uses a urine flask from the medicine chest to give a sample. The barber surgeon holds it up to the light and examines its colour. He then smells the mouth of the flask and, dipping his finger in it, tastes the urine. Now he can tell what is wrong with the sailor.

▶ Two doctors examine a urine flask in 1518.

▲ This stained-glass window shows St Cosmas with a urine flask and surgeon's knife.

The different sections of the urine flask represented different parts of the body. The doctor examined the superior or top section for illness in the head and brain. He looked at the middle section for signs of disease in the heart, lungs and stomach. The inferior or bottom section was studied for problems below the waist. There were thirty different signs of disease, including colour, smell and taste.

◀ A Tudor urine flask.

◄ This cartoon from 1520 makes fun of the doctor's urine flask.

Feverfew dried and made into pouder, and taken with hony or sweet wine, purgeth melancholy and flegme; wherefore it is very good for them that are giddie in the head.

Someone's personality depended on which of the four 'humours' they had most of in their body. They might be:
sanguine (warm and cheerful)
phlegmatic (cool and sluggish)
melancholic (gloomy and sad)
bilious (ill-natured and quick-tempered).

Tudor doctors believed that the body was made up of four different 'humours' or fluids – blood, phlegm, black bile and yellow bile. Having too much of one humour was thought to cause illness and bad moods. By examining a patient's urine flask carefully, the doctor was able to tell which humour was causing the trouble.

The humours could be balanced by following a special diet. The doctor advised children to eat cool, moist foods like cheese and milk to control their phlegm.

► A fifteenth-century diagram from the Book of the Barber Surgeons of York, showing the characters of the four humours as different people.

CUPS AND LEECHES

GIVING BLOOD

The surgeon says he must bleed the sailor, to remove the bad humours from his body. He places a cup containing a burning rag over a wound on the sailor's back. As the rag burns, the cup bites into his skin and sucks out a stream of yellow pus. With his scalpel, the surgeon cuts a vein in the sailor's foot, spraying out a fountain of scarlet blood which he catches in a large bowl.

▲ A pewter bleeding bowl from the medicine chest on the *Mary Rose*.

If you visited a Tudor doctor, he was very likely to attach leeches to your skin – to suck out the 'bad blood' believed to cause disease. Leeches have suckers containing sharp teeth which can bite through the flesh. They also dribble a special saliva which stops the bite from hurting and prevents the blood from clotting. They can happily slurp up nearly five times their own body weight, and are still used today in some surgical operations.

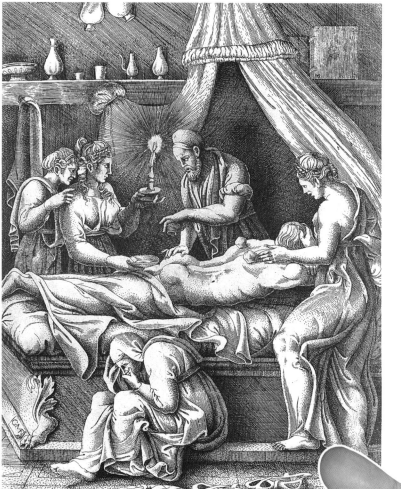

▼ A sixteenth-century doctor 'cupping' his patient.

▼ A leech at work.

For headache and madness open veins in the back of the neck.

For ailment of the mouth or toothache open two veins below the tongue.

◀ A patient with leeches on his arm, in a medical text from 1560.

Leeches were sold to the doctor by professional leech-catchers. They could be left to wriggle in jars in the medicine chest, because they need to feed only once every few months.

Tudor doctors happily used cups, scalpels and leeches to drain large amounts of blood from their poor patients, whatever their illness. Different complaints were treated by bleeding from different parts of the body. Bleeding from the feet was carried out in the belief that this drew the blood containing the 'bad humours' downwards, away from the brain and heart.

Medicine was based as much on superstition as science. Doctors decided which vein to open only after checking a patient's birth-date and star sign. The best day for a bleeding depended on the size and position of the moon.

▶ This 1508 chart shows which bleeding points belong to which star sign.

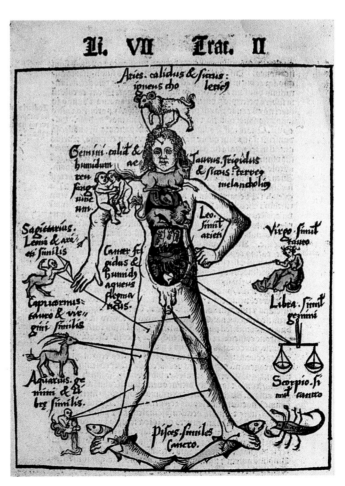

CURES FROM PLANTS

After studying a large, dusty book, the barber surgeon pours a selection of dried herbs from his medicine jars into a leather pouch. 'Take these morning and evening, boiled with a little sugar,' he tells the trembling sailor, who is pale after giving so much blood.

▼ The front page of John Gerarde's Herbal, published in 1597.

▶ Rosemary, lavender and bay leaves were all used in Tudor medicines.

Tudor doctors looked up cures in books called 'herbals', like the one written by barber surgeon John Gerarde in 1597. Below are some of his recipes:

'The heads of poppie boiled in water with a little sugar to a syrrup cause sleepe, and are good against rheumes [colds], and catarrhes.'

▼ A recipe using cherries in a herbal from 1545.

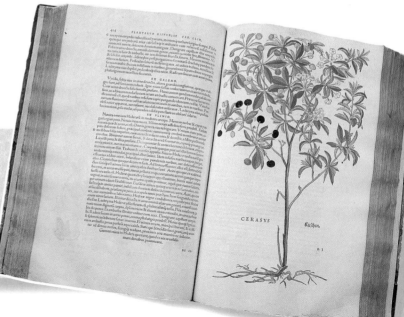

'The distilled water of the floures of Rosemary being drunke at morning and evening first and last, taketh away the stench of the mouth and breath, and maketh it very sweet, if there be added thereto ... a few Cloves, Mace, Cinnamon, and a little Annise seed.'

Doctors believed that plants looked like the illnesses which they could cure. Jaundice, which turns the skin yellow, was treated with yellow flowers. Red flowers were thought to purify the blood. Heart disease was treated with leaves shaped like hearts. When Queen Elizabeth I suffered from smallpox, which causes a red rash, doctors decorated her bedroom in red!

To cure baldness, anoint the head with the grease of a fox...wash the head with the juice of beets five or six times or else stamp garlic and rub the head with it, and after that wash it with vinegar.

◀ Poppies, which contain opium, are used in both Tudor and modern medicines.

▲ A doctor attends his patient in 1600, while his helper makes a cure from bark.

Most herbal remedies, though, were based on a long history of successful use. Modern doctors treat some illnesses with chemicals taken from the same plants that Tudor doctors used.

▲ Ointment canisters from the Mary Rose.

POWDERED MICE

EARACHE

Waiting for his next patient, the surgeon grinds up mice bones with a mortar and pestle. He mixes in honey and oil of roses, then pours his new cure into a jar marked 'Earache'.

▼ A book of cures from 1530.

▲ An ear operation in 1524.

'To cure deafness, put nothing on to the ear except it be as warm as blood. Then take the gall of an hare and mix it with the grease of a fox and with blade well instil it into the ear.'

Each doctor's medicine chest held his own favourite cures. Many had strange and revolting ingredients, based on magic and superstition rather than knowledge.

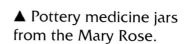

▲ Pottery medicine jars from the *Mary Rose*.

14

To cure warts, lay half a mouse on the wart for half an hour and then bury it in the ground. As the mouse rots the wart will disappear.

◄ A doctor prepares his ingredients.

Mice were prescribed for all kinds of illness. They were easily obtained and quite pleasant to eat! Mice were roasted or fried with onions, as cures for consumption and whooping cough. They were burnt to a cinder, then mixed with jam as a cure for bed-wetting. A doctor's medicine jars were full of various mice remedies.

▲ Imagine having to take medicine made from mice!

Mice Remedies

Gout: Mice cut in two and laid on the feet or legs of those who are gouty is an excellent remedy and cure for them.
Earache: The dust and powder of mice being mixed with honey and oil of roses and afterwards diluted into a clear water. Then pour into the ears of anyone who is deaf and troubled with any pain in the ears.
Scouring the teeth: The heads of mice being burned and beaten into powder is excellent for the scouring and cleansing of the teeth. This powder is called 'Toothsoap'.

SPIDERS AND COBWEBS

WHOOPING COUGH

When a young girl enters the surgery complaining of 'shivery ague', the surgeon lifts a jar of live spiders from the medicine chest. Dipping one in butter, he places it, still wriggling, on the poor girl's tongue. Holding her nose, she gulps it down. 'The wriggling of the spider,' says the surgeon, 'will cure the shivering of the ague.'

Spiders were a popular medicine. They were swallowed alive or trapped in nutshells to be worn around the neck. Their webs were used to stop nosebleeds and heal wounds. Webs were also laid over sores to draw out poison. Modern research has shown that cobwebs actually contain a powerful antiseptic.

◄ Spiders, scorpions and other creepy-crawlies were used in many popular cures.

Unlike today, children were not vaccinated against killer diseases such as whooping cough. The many youngsters infected by this illness also had to suffer the revolting cures offered by Tudor doctors. Look inside a Tudor medicine chest and you will see many strange whooping cough remedies.

To cure whooping cough, find a ferret, give it milk to drink and then feed what is left to the sick child.

◀ A hooting owl was believed to cure whooping cough.

An old Sussex whooping cough cure was to drink a broth made from owls. Remedies were based on their similarity to the illness. Just as a wriggly spider was used to treat shivery ague, so a hooting owl and a braying donkey were believed to have power over the whooping of the child's cough.

▶ Passing a child under and over a donkey was another whooping cough cure.

Whooping Cough Cures

- Swing the child upwards by the heels.
- Take a spoonful of woodlice, bruise them, mix with breast milk and take for three or four mornings.
- Drink broth, liquor or syrup made from snails.
- Take a child to a barn and let him breathe in the breath of cattle, sheep or horses.

PLIERS

TOOTHACHE

The barber surgeon takes some pliers from his medicine chest. An actor from the local theatre has toothache. A scream pierces the surgery as the surgeon yanks out the bad tooth.

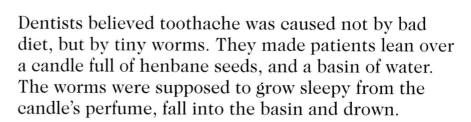

◄ Removing the worms that cause toothache!

◄ A Tudor dentist at work with his pliers.

Dentists believed toothache was caused not by bad diet, but by tiny worms. They made patients lean over a candle full of henbane seeds, and a basin of water. The worms were supposed to grow sleepy from the candle's perfume, fall into the basin and drown.

▼ There was no privacy at this seventeenth century dentist's!

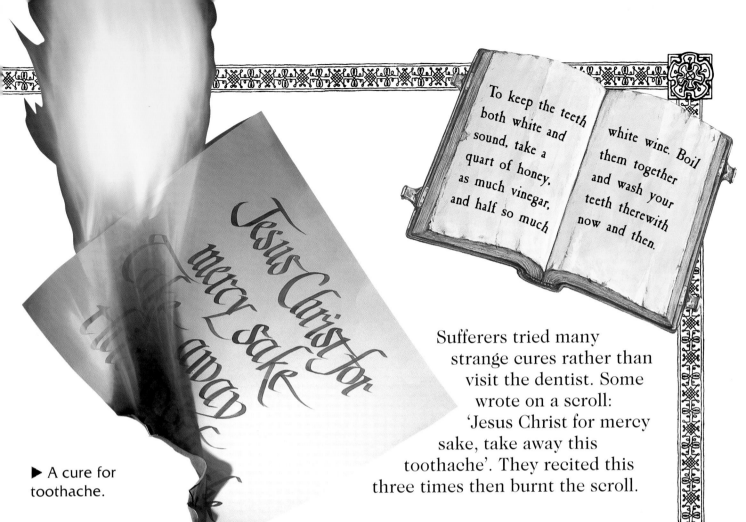

To keep the teeth both white and sound, take a quart of honey, as much vinegar, and half so much white wine. Boil them together and wash your teeth therewith now and then.

Sufferers tried many strange cures rather than visit the dentist. Some wrote on a scroll: 'Jesus Christ for mercy sake, take away this toothache'. They recited this three times then burnt the scroll.

▶ A cure for toothache.

Tudor barbers were not only surgeons but dentists. They did not know how to make fillings, so if your toothache became unbearable they simply pulled out the bad tooth. There were no injections to numb the mouth, so loud screams were often heard coming from the barbers.

▶ A sixteenth-century diagram of the jaw and teeth, by the artist Leonardo da Vinci.

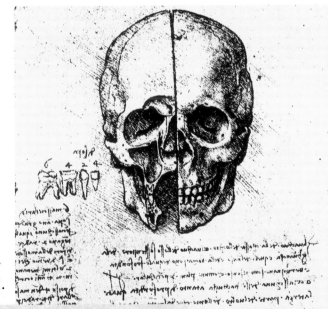

'Take a garlic head, beat it in a mortar that it wax soft: and look on what side or cheek the toothache is. On that arm bind the garlic upon the wrist. Cover it with a broad walnut shell a whole night, and then it will cast a blister: pierce the same through, or else it will burst by itself. That healeth the tooth.'

SAW

SURGERY

An assistant enters the room as the surgeon lifts a large saw from his medicine chest. A soldier's wounded leg is infected with gangrene, and must be amputated. The assistant punches the terrified soldier unconscious, then holds him down as the saw's teeth start to bite into his leg.

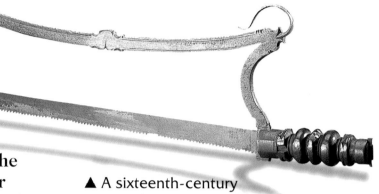

▲ A sixteenth-century surgeon's amputation saw.

◀ ▼ This Tudor tapestry and drawing fail to show the terrible pain of amputation.

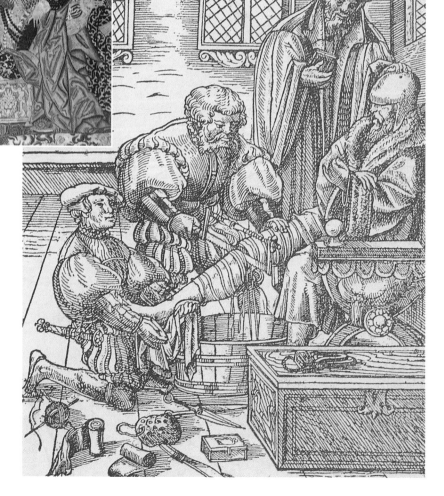

The Tudor surgeon operated to remove diseased limbs. He worked in his everyday, blood-stained clothes, and left his surgical instruments lying on the dirty floor. Despite sniffing opium-soaked sponges or drinking alcohol, the patient suffered terribly. Several men held the victim down while the surgeon sawed. Loss of blood, or infection from the filthy surgery often resulted in the patient's agonizing death.

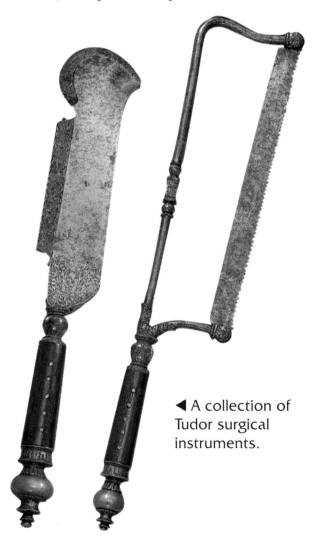

To cure gout, take a frog when neither sun nor moon is shining: cut off its hind legs and wrap them in deer skin. Apply the right to the right and the left to the left foot of the gouty person and without doubt he will be healed.

The same tools used to butcher a deer were used to perform surgery. There were instruments for sawing, cutting, gripping and probing. Look inside a Tudor medicine chest and you will see saws, knives, clamps, hooks, scalpels and probes.

▲ This 1597 drawing shows an example of Tudor cosmetic surgery – a nose-job!

◄ A collection of Tudor surgical instruments.

SYRINGE

MILITARY SURGEONS

An iron rod and a flask of oil from the medicine chest are heated over a fire. Having finished the amputation, the surgeon presses the red-hot iron against the bloody wound. Then he pours on the boiling oil, which hisses and smokes as the bleeding slows to a trickle.

► This sixteenth-century trepan was used to pierce the skull in early brain surgery.

▲ A surgeon in 1600 using a trepan.

One of the most terrifying instruments in the medicine chest was the 'cautery', a red-hot iron used to stop bleeding and treat disease. Another dreadful implement was the 'trepan'. This was used to drill holes in the skull, a practice started in prehistoric times to release evil spirits from the brain. Imagine going to the doctor with a head-ache, and seeing him pick up his drill!

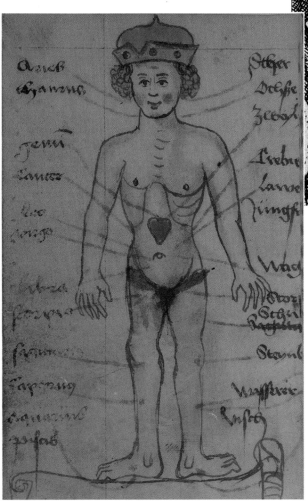

◄ Doctors treated disease by applying red-hot cauteries to points shown on their charts.

Medical advances were being made by military surgeons. A French army surgeon called Ambrose Pare saw that treating open wounds with the agonizing cautery and boiling oil caused inflammation and fever. He discovered that applying dressings with a mixture of eggs, oil of roses and turpentine was far more successful. When he had cured a soldier, he would say: 'I dressed him; God healed him.'

To cure the headache burn or dry the skin of a mouse, beat into a powder and mingle with vinegar.

Anoint the head of anyone who is pained. It will ease and help him.

▲ A military surgery in the sixteenth century.

Increasing knowledge moved medicine away from superstition towards science. Two syringes found in the medicine chest of the *Mary Rose* look very similar to the syringes your doctor might use today.

▲ A syringe used by the surgeon on the Mary Rose.

SCALPEL

CUTTING UP CORPSES

A fresh corpse is carried into the surgery. Shut away on his own, the surgeon takes a scalpel and makes a deep cut along the corpse's chest. He pulls back the warm flesh and peers inside. Grasping a blood-spattered notebook, the surgeon scribbles down a sketch of what he sees.

▲ Andreas Vesalius dissecting a corpse.

◀ An illustration from On the Fabric of the Human Body, published by Vesalius in 1543.

New medical knowledge was based on doctors using scalpels to dissect and observe human corpses. The Belgian professor Andreas Vesalius snatched corpses from the gallows while writing the first accurate book of anatomy, *On the Fabric of the Human Body*. Leonardo da Vinci created detailed drawings of human anatomy after dissecting over thirty corpses.

◀ Tudor scalpels.

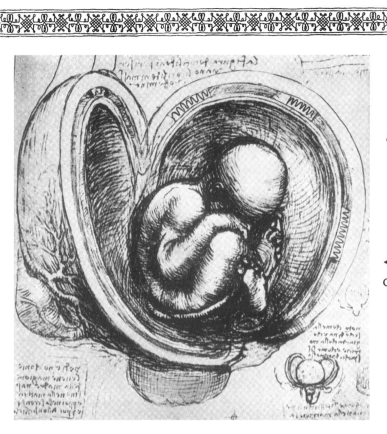

For the pain in the ears, take three live spiders, boil them with oil upon the fire, then distil or drop a little of this oil into the pained ear.

◀ Da Vinci's drawing of a child in the womb.

In England, Henry VIII gave barber surgeons permission to dissect the bodies of just four criminals each year. The Royal College of Surgeons was founded in Henry's reign, but it wasn't until 1565 that Elizabeth I granted the college the right to practise regular dissections.

FIGVRA PRIMA

▲ A 1600 study of a dissected neck.

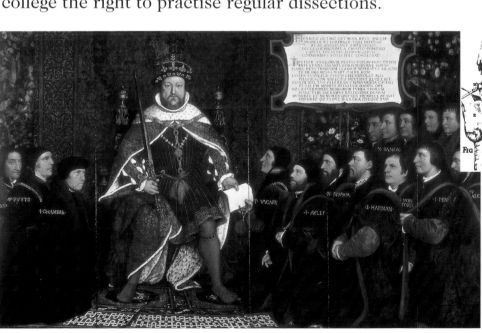

◀ Henry VIII creating the Royal Guild of Barber Surgeons in 1541.

THE PLAGUE

From outside the surgery comes a cry of 'Plague!' With trembling hands, the surgeon reaches into his medicine chest and lifts out gloves and a heavy cloak. He picks up a strange mask, with a beak at the front which he stuffs full of sweet-smelling herbs. Putting on this plague outfit, the surgeon looks like some sort of monstrous, nightmare bird.

In 1563, 17,000 people died from plague in London alone. Frightened children clasped hands and sang the nursery rhyme 'Ring a ring of roses', which is about the plague.

'Ring a ring of roses,
A pocketful of posies,
Atishoo, atishoo,
We all fall down.'

◀ A doctor dressed to treat victims of plague.

A plague victim's body was covered with red boils that looked like a 'ring of roses'. People carried 'posies' of flowers in their pockets, to cover up the stench of rotting corpses. Sneezing was a sign that you had the plague, and might be dead within a day – 'We all fall down'. Believing the disease to be punishment from God, people whipped themselves in the streets to seek forgiveness for their sins.

◀ Victims seek God's forgiveness.

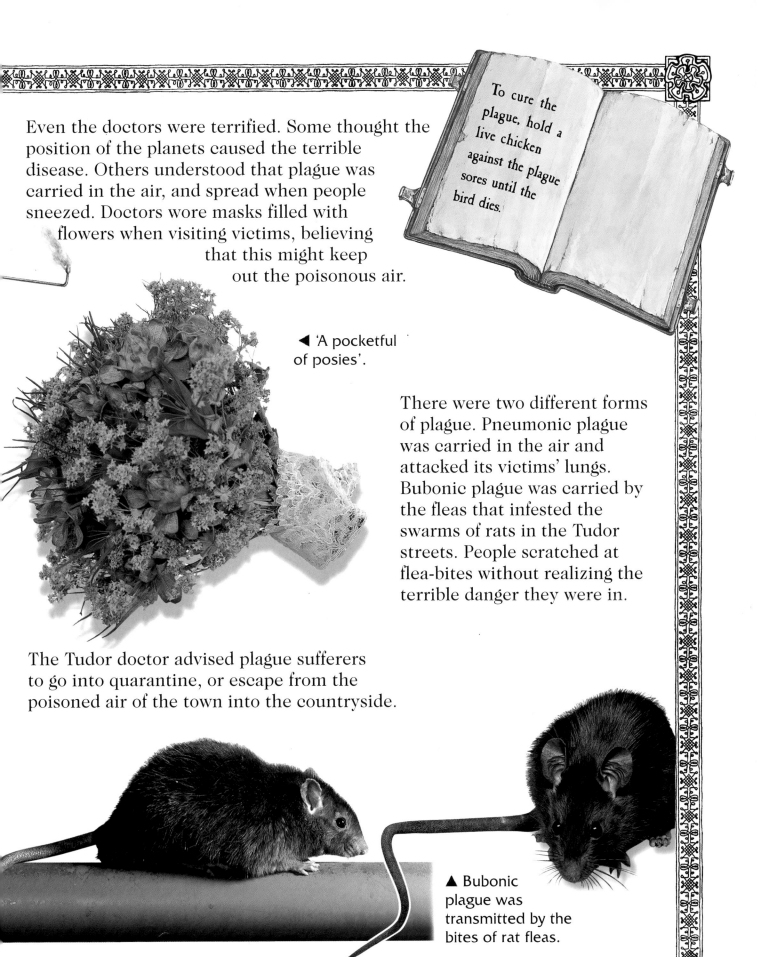

Even the doctors were terrified. Some thought the position of the planets caused the terrible disease. Others understood that plague was carried in the air, and spread when people sneezed. Doctors wore masks filled with flowers when visiting victims, believing that this might keep out the poisonous air.

To cure the plague, hold a live chicken against the plague sores until the bird dies.

◄ 'A pocketful of posies'.

There were two different forms of plague. Pneumonic plague was carried in the air and attacked its victims' lungs. Bubonic plague was carried by the fleas that infested the swarms of rats in the Tudor streets. People scratched at flea-bites without realizing the terrible danger they were in.

The Tudor doctor advised plague sufferers to go into quarantine, or escape from the poisoned air of the town into the countryside.

▲ Bubonic plague was transmitted by the bites of rat fleas.

PLAGUE CAUTERY

PIERCING BUBOES

A merchant staggers into the surgery and tears open his tunic. Pus-filled, purple boils cover his swollen armpits. Snatching a long-handled cautery from the medicine chest, the surgeon heats it in the fire. At arm's-length, he presses its red-hot tip against a bubo which explodes with a hiss.

◄ Priests used this dispenser to give plague victims holy water and wafers.

► A long-handled plague cautery.

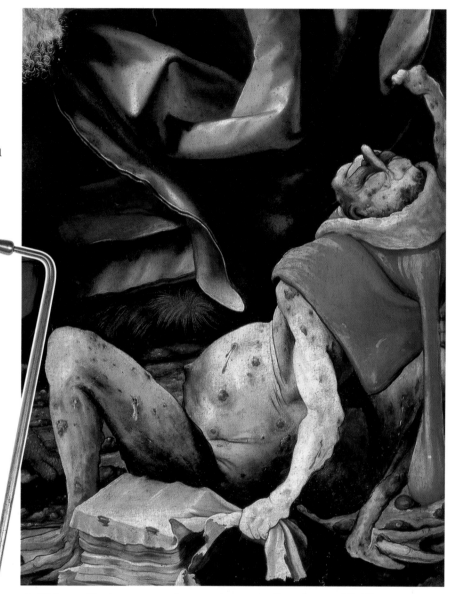

▲ This suffering man decorates an altar from 1510.

If you saw dark swellings called 'buboes' around your arm-pits, you knew that you had the plague. Doctors pierced buboes with a long-handled cautery, to try to destroy the poison. The handle meant they didn't have to get too close to the highly infectious patient. Priests nervously gave holy water and wafers to dying victims with a dispenser which had a long handle for the same purpose.

Desperate plague victims tried many different cures:

- Roasted onions filled with treacle and pepper made into a poultice.
- Dried toads laid on the buboes to draw out the poison.
- A mixture of onions, cloves, garlic, lemons and vinegar.

To cure the plague, take two pounds of figs, two handfuls of rue and sixty walnuts beaten small, then use as a poultice to draw out the poison.

Tudor doctors tried all manner of remedies, but nothing in the medicine chest could stop the plague from taking its many victims to an early grave.

▼ A fifteenth-century charm supposed to keep plague away.

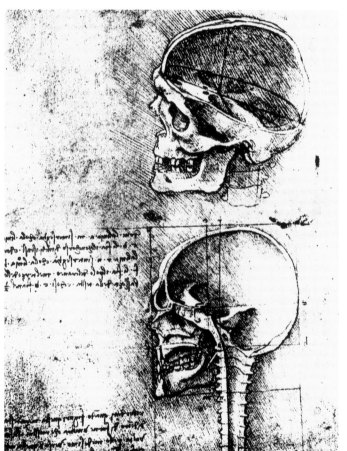

▲ No charms or cures could save a plague victim.

'If a man be sick of a fever, it is some comfort that he can take a bedstaff and knock, and his servant comes up and helps him ... But if a man be sick of the plague, then he sits and dies all alone.'

GLOSSARY

Anaemia A medical condition that makes you look pale and tired, caused by having too few red blood cells.

Anaesthetic A substance that dulls pain.

Anatomy The science that deals with the physical structure of humans, animals and plants.

Anoint Smear or rub with something.

Antiseptic Substance that kills germs and infections.

Appendicitis A painful illness caused by infection of the appendix.

Consumption A lung disorder leading to a wasting away of the body.

Dissect Cut up something so that it can be examined more closely.

Dysentery An infectious disease causing diarrhoea.

Glands Cells or organs in the body that create substances vital to the body.

Gout A disease that causes painful swelling of joints, especially of the toe and foot.

Henbane A poisonous plant with sticky, hairy leaves.

Malaria A serious disease caused by mosquito bites.

Mortar A bowl used with a pestle to grind spices and other substances into smaller pieces.

Opium The dried juice of the opium poppy, containing the pain-killer, morphine.

Palpitations Rapid beating of the heart.

Poultice A pad with ointment on it that soothes sore and swollen parts of the body.

Purge Get rid of, purify.

Quack A person who pretends to be a doctor but is not qualified.

Quarantine A period of time that a person has to spend alone to stop the spread of disease.

Rue A strongly scented plant with bitter-tasting leaves.

Vaccinated Injected with a medicine that protects you from disease.

FURTHER READING

Mountfield, Anne *Looking Back at Medicine* (Macmillan, 1988)

Parker, Steve *Medicine (Eyewitness Science)* (Dorling Kindersley, 1995)

Parker, Steve *The Human Body (Eyewitness Science)* (Dorling Kindersley, 1993)

Senior, Kathryn *Medicine: Doctors, Demons and Drugs* (Watts Books, 1993)

Triggs, Tony *Scientists and Writers (Tudors and Stuarts)* (Wayland, 1993)

The Tudor cures quoted in this book were taken from a number of sources including:
Allen, Andrew *A Dictionary of Sussex Folk Medicine* (Countryside Books, 1995)
Boorde, Andrew *Breviary of Helthe* (1547)
Camp, John *Magic, Myth and Medicine* (Priory Press, 1973)
Gerard, John *Gerard's Herbal* (1597)
Topsell, Rev. Edward *The Book of Four-Footed Beasts and Serpents and Insects* (1658)

INDEX

Numbers in **bold** refer to pictures.